LIVING YOUR PURPOSE

Nuggets for a joyful pursuit of purpose

Veronica Ngina Kanja

LIVING YOUR PURPOSE

Published by

P. O. Box 4865-00506
Nairobi, Kenya.
Cell phone: 0748 227 571/0729 368 307
Email: nenopublisher@gmail.com,
info@nenopublishers.co.ke
Website: www.nenopublishers.co.ke

ISBN 13: 978-9914-9884-5-1

Printed in Kenya

Table of Contents

Dedication

This book is dedicated to you, the reader. It is an honour that you have chosen to read it. The book has been written to inspire and encourage you as you soldier on the journey of living your purpose and pursuing of greatness. It will remind you that no matter what you go through, that is not the end. God has planned something great in your life. He must complete and see you through to the end. It is not yet done until it is done!

Acknowledgements

In a special way, I want to acknowledge my parents, Grace, and Simon for their tremendous support to my work and their constant encouragement throughout this journey.

My gratitude also goes to my sister and brother, Rita and Martin, for their inspiration in their own little ways, as I always strive to set a good example as their eldest sister.

Thanks to my entire family and good friends, for their generous support and encouragement. Their role was significant in fulfilling my hope of writing this book.

Thanks to my mentors for their exemplary motivation and constant encouragement in my quest to accomplish my purpose.

Many thanks, to everyone who has been resourceful throughout all the stages of publishing this book, including editing, designing and printing.

Most importantly, I thank God for his abundant grace upon me. He has remained my inspiration through his constant encouragement from his word while in the pursuit of my dream in life. I thank Him, whom, through His grace I stand, for giving me the strength to write this book.

To God be the glory.

Inspirational Corner

Remember to look up at the stars and not down at your feet. Try to make sense of what you see and wonder about what makes the universe exist. Be curious. However difficult life may seem, there is always something you can do and succeed at. It matters that you don't just give up. - By Stephen Hawking

Great things are not done by impulse but by a series of small things brought together. I am still far from being what I want to be, but with God's help I shall succeed." Then let us keep courage and try to be patient and gentle. The beginning is perhaps more difficult than anything else, but keep heart, it will turn out alright. The heart of man is very much like the sea, it has its storms, it has its tides, and, in its depths, it has its pearls too. Your profession is not what brings your weekly paycheck, your profession is what you are put here on earth to do, with such passion and such intensity that it becomes spiritual in calling. - (Vincent Van Gogh).

"When I got enough confidence, the stage was gone... When I was sure I was losing, I won. When I needed people the most, they left me. When I learnt to dry my tears, I found a shoulder to cry on. When I mastered the skill of hating, someone started loving me from the core of the heart and, while waiting for the light for hours, when I fell

asleep, the sun came out. That is LIFE! No matter what you plan, you never know what life has planned for you. Success introduces you to the world. But failure introduces the world to you. Always be Happy! Often when we lose Hope and think this is the end, God smiles from above and says, Relax Sweetheart; It's just a BEND! Not the END!" (Sophia Loren).

Life offers more when purpose is our focus. This purpose driven focus propels us past challenges, pains, and shortcuts and even what might appear in our eyes as failure. On deeper reflections, we understand these challenges as catalysts that shift us towards authentic self-identity, greater exposure, and bold life adventures. -TD Jakes

If I fail, I try again, and again. The human spirit can handle much worse than we realize. It matters how you are going to finish not how you start. Are you going to finish strong? -Nick Vujicic.

Introduction

Value yourself

Waking up every morning is a miracle, no matter the condition you are in. The fact that you still have life guarantees that you have another chance of giving life another try. If you are still breathing, you still have a mission to hold on to the fight and finish the race.

Your purpose is that inner compass that leads you into fulfilling your ultimate destiny. We were created to be useful to the world and this is achieved through purposeful living. Living purposefully has been defined as one of the most effortful but enjoyable experiences that we get to experience in our lives. Purpose, in most cases is referred to as the reason for which something (someone) exists or is created for. Pre-designed purpose then, in this case, would mean that our lives have been designed beforehand or in advance, for a reason or purpose to be fulfilled.

The purpose for a bicycle is different from that of a motorcycle, an air vessel or a marine vessel. In the normal circumstances, it would be absurd for a person to use airplane on a highway, or a motorcycle in the water or a bicycle on the railway. Each of them was made for a specific purpose. In the same way, we are made for different purposes, which we must pursue to accomplish.

We must aspire to try being better by working on ourselves even if we can't see any results yet. We should live a step at a time, because we may never know what results may come out of our actions. Conversely, it is certain that if we do nothing, certainly there will be no results- Mahatma Gandhi

A renowned Italian painter and artist, Leonardo da Vinci once said, *"Iron rusts from disuse, stagnant water loses its purity, and in cold weather becomes frozen, even so does inaction sap the vigor of the mind"*. This illustrates how inactivity can be detrimental to our lives. We need to keep moving no matter what comes our way. Inaction or passiveness is dangerous. Regardless of the results, we need to keep trying always until something different happens or changes.

My Story

I got some 'Aha' moments while I was in the process of searching and trying to find out my own purpose. It was a long search and a struggle, trying to get the reason why God created me. This was a point where, nothing mattered to me - nothing impressed me. Life had lost its meaning to me. For that reason, I had to look for the reason why I was still alive every day that I opened my eyes, every single morning. I did not know why at my age, I still had not known the purpose for my life. Sometimes I blamed it on God why He had hidden it from me.

One day I resorted to research for it. I looked for articles and books on purpose in the same way a school project is done in school or how research is done in a research center. Then, I pieced most of the information I got into little notes, which later, I compiled to make a book. This was with a view that in case I found helpful information on life's purpose I could help someone else or many others to discover their purpose as well.

What I figured out is that, a person who resolves to search for answers on purpose, may not be a happy person, and might be a confused one. This was exactly what I was going through at that point in my life. I was in a state of confusion, almost depressed and with occasional moments of despair. Thank God, I did not bend too low to the challenges.

I had just come back from abroad after spending some years there while studying. I hoped that coming back would be a good fresh start for me. I needed to find a job immediately since I had not saved enough at that moment for an entrepreneurship venture. At that moment, I thought how easy it would be to spring back into the busy life of the city and run the normal errands like everyone else - but I was wrong. Adjusting to the life of the country, especially at a time when Kenya was going through a series of difficult economic times was not easy. During that time, every citizen was tired of hearing about corruption, hunger in different parts of the country and cases of homicides as the everyday breaking news. It was also challenging adjusting to the social life, after being away for so long. Another thing that was difficult was meeting people's expectations of me now that I was back home. For sure, it was not an easy time.

These are the challenges that many people face when they go back to their home countries after a long period abroad. Not many people are willing to talk about their experiences after their return home. People will assume that you are okay and have everything figured out. They believe that you came back home with a good plan for your ventures and their solutions as well. Well, some people go back home well prepared but a good number too, still struggle trying to figure out themselves in these situations. Many of these people come back with good intentions of applying the skills and knowledge learnt abroad for the good of their own countries. Then, reality hits them and they go for months without jobs. Some do not get support for creating their start-up companies. Some suffer from depression and experience difficulties as a result of social alienation. They are not able to fit well in the social circles. Some people will even point out that you might be lying when you acknowlege of not being okay or not financially stable.

There are so many misconceptions about people coming back to the country from abroad, whether they were studying or working. People will expect you to behave as if you have your life all figured out, without even wanting to know what kind of life you lived or what you went through while living abroad. Many years back, I heard stories of people who came back home after many years of living abroad. Some became sick, depressed and others developed mental illnesses due to the adjustment they had to make, which was not smooth especially for those that had not prepared effectively in advance for their return home. I thought that these stories of people having depression upon returning home after years abroad were not real until I experienced it myself. Since then, I have always advocated to support that category of people emotionally, psychologically, in social circles, in support groups and also financially for those in difficult financial constraints considering that these people really experience different problems in the life outside their motherland.

Let me take you back to my story after returning home. In the process of trying to adapt to a different system once again I slowly fell into depression. I was not the same person who had left. So many things had changed in me. I had travelled a lot, I got the opportunity of having new and mind-blowing experiences. I had achieved a lot. I had also failed many times and had lots of challenges out of my native motherland.

When I came back, nothing much had changed, from my hometown to the city, apart from some new roads that had been partially completed and other new and beautiful buildings that had been completed.

I was worried about where my life was heading to. I watched videos of how some students had left for studies abroad. When they came back home, they were successful in getting jobs immediately which helped them adapt to the system and also get into social circles smoothly. On the contrary, my situation was different. I waited for so many months without a job, apart from the occasional interviews that I attended after submitting many job applications. As a result of what I was going through, I also became antisocial. I gradually moved away from the few old friends whom we had both hoped to reconnect after my return. In my mind I would be thinking about the little chitchat that would start with something like "*So, what have you been up to since you came back*?" I was not ready to answer such questions. I had also made up my mind to give up on employment and venture into a startup company with the idea that I had in mind. However, I felt like I didn't have enough capital for the startup and my mind was still not stable. I was not mentally prepared at that moment to go into agreements with financial institutions to provide the capital.

This also made me think of how life would have been for me if I had not left my country. The colleagues I had left behind seemed to be doing very well in their careers. Life seemed to have turned out really good for them. At that time, I was now blaming God why He let me leave the country to go and experience new opportunities and then come back to my motherland to suffer. It was so confusing. I neither understood what God was really doing with my life nor His purpose for me. I didn't understand that sometimes God has to work on you as a person before working on your situation. Life was all crazy for me then. However, I was determined to adjust to my new reality in each way that I could. In addition, this challenging experience, enabled me to look at life's issues in a different perspective, later on in life. I kept on reading inspirational and motivational books. I went for life-changing and spiritual retreats to get the encouragement that I needed. Occasionally, I would break down and start the adjusting cycle all over again.

Upon reading deeply and trying to search for answers through the crisis that I was going through, I finally came to the realization that our destinies had already been defined or designed even before we were born. We are only required **to discover our purpose** and what we were intended to do on earth after our creation. At the end, it will not matter anymore how long it took us to know and discover ourselves and our purpose better, as long as we have already discovered what connects us to our destiny. Something else that is quite intriguing is that we will keep learning new things about ourselves every year until the day we die. As I sit down on my desktop typing this, I am proud to say that the time you think was wasted, was not at all wasted. You will figure out what you have been looking for all this time! You were already "**designed for a purpose**!"

1

SELF-IDENTITY

Self-identity is the first step to discover your purpose.

Self-identity is the knowledge of our personality attributes, qualities, expressions, natural abilities, skills and acquired abilities. Discovering our identity gives us the ability to seek our true purpose and personal fulfillment. Discovering oneself is a journey that takes long to be fully accomplished. From knowing our identities, we start a long-lasting journey of developing capabilities to know ourselves better each day. Try to observe your habits, patterns, and character. Find out what triggers you, what your dreams are, what your ambitions are and what generally drives you. Acknowledge your fears and failures. Examine yourself and see how these fears and failures can be transformed to be your motivation in life. Then, start working on them day by day to be a better version of yourself.

"Purpose is an essential element of you. It is the reason you are on the planet at this particular time in history. Your very existence is wrapped up in the things you are here on earth to fulfill-Chadwick Boseman

Many are the times we are asked to introduce ourselves to people, describing who we are and what we do in life. On many occasions, this could be in a group, an association or even during a job interview. We can always find the words to describe who we are depending on the situation or audience. You might answer the questions about who you are very eloquently and impressively. However, it is good to pause and ask yourself whether you are sure of whom your creator says you are.

Getting to know yourself better is always a process that involves a series of steps directed towards achieving what you really want in life. One thing that is important to keep in mind is that, whom you say you are, matters more than who people say you are. *"While you are walking on your journey, your God's calling, your passion or your purpose, you're going to have to take that walk alone, sometimes."*- Lisa Nichols

"He knows the plans he has for us which are not to harm, but to give hope and a future." It is not what people say that defines us, but what we say about ourselves and ultimately what God says about us. *"He knows the plans he has for us which are not to harm, but to give hope and a future."*

Take care of yourself

If you have a purpose to achieve, you will need to check on your welfare. Do you love yourself enough? Do you take good care of yourself enough? Do you consistently nourish your body with the right foods to keep you healthy and strong as long as God keeps you? "We are what we eat". The prevention of lifestyle diseases through healthy eating and physical exercise cannot be overemphasized. Remember that you have an impact on your family and those around you. "*You become an average of the five people that you spend most of your time with*". If for instance you begin the habit of healthy eating, you will be surprised by how much that can influence on the eating habits of your family and friends too. Mind energies are infectious and it is critical that

We are what we eat

we are conscious to hang around more with people that lead more positive and healthy lifestyles because we unconsciously attract and imitate habits from each other. It is therefore essential that we also take care of ourselves mentally, spiritually and socially in this matter.

In our society today, there are many cases of people suffering from depression, for reasons such as social pressures brought about by social media among other factors. Other issues on the rise are like domestic and family conflicts that negatively affects the lives of people. You need to love and accept yourself even if there are issues that you cannot change about yourself such as your family background, relatives et al. Loving ourselves coupled with self-knowledge of who we are as individuals, makes us capable of trusting ourselves that we have the best interest at heart for ourselves. This makes us confident in the pursuit for our purpose.

"God grant me the Serenity to accept the things I cannot change, Courage to change the things I can and Wisdom to know the difference."
Lord make me an instrument of your peace
Where there is hatred let me bring love
Where there is doubt, let me bring faith
Where there is despair let me bring hope
Where there is darkness let me bring light
Where there is sadness let me bring joy
O divine master grant that I may
Not so much seek to be consoled as to console
To be understood as to understand
To be loved as to love
For it is in pardoning that we are pardoned
And it's in dying that we are born to eternal life
Amen - Prayer of St. Francis of Assisi

When you need help or counsel, seek a counselor or somebody with prudence that can help you out. Seek God and let him take control over your life.

> *"You were made by God and for God, and until you understand that, life will never make sense."*

It may be difficult to discover our purpose in life without having a spiritual grounding to base ourselves on. **"You were made by God and for God, and until you understand that, life will never make sense"** - **Rick Warren**. Our creator, created every one of us with a purpose.

Then it is our duty to find out why He did create us. *"Before I formed you in the womb, I knew you."* (Jer 1:5)

"I have loved you with an everlasting love." (Jer 31:3) ***I will not leave you nor forget you, like a mother does not forget her child and if she forgets, I will not forget you."*** (Isaiah 49) **"Those who hope in me shall never be disappointed."**

Self-care and self-love is important but should not be confused with selfishness or lack of empathy to others. We should be generous and show love to one another as God has commanded us. The youth are advised not to waste their youthfulness but instead, they should   make the best out of the time they have - keeping in mind that there is a time for everything. We are required to grab every good opportunity that knocks on our doors, to follow our aspirations, dreams, hopes, goals, and the desires of our hearts; remembering that God will judge our motives. Ecclesiastes 11:9

Wash before you return!

In the ancient times, the youthful days of our grandparents, people borrowed items such as clothes and shoes from each other to attend ceremonies or when travelling. The interesting thing is that when it was time to return the items to their owners, the borrowers would clean them so much that they would be cleaner than how they borrowed from their owners.

In the same way, our souls, spirits, and bodies also have been given temporarily by the sole owner -God, who has the power to take them back when He is pleased. Therefore, it is always our duty to use these three entities, soul, spirit, and body, for their intended purpose on earth and to return them back better than how He gave us since the time of our conception. We can give them back better than how He gave to us. This can be through knowing Him better through our acts of kindness to one another.

We also need to use the gifts and talents that He has given us to better and change our lives and the lives of others for His greater glory.

Write down your vision

Write down your vision and clearly inscribe it on the tablets so that he may run who reads it. Habakkuk 2:2 We need to write down our plans and visions for us to remain committed to them. Writing down our goals helps us to remember that they are important and achievable to us. It makes our minds focus on the importance of accomplishing them. Thinking of the daily-to-do lists clearly makes us focus on achieving our daily tasks effectively. When we don't put these visions down, we quickly tend to forget and assume that they are of less importance. Writing creates a path for implementation.

Moses was instructed by God to write down the ten commandments on stone tablets. By writing them down, the Israelites would read, remember, memorize, follow and implement the commandments in their daily living.

Writing creates a path for implementation.

"*Write in a book all the words that I have spoken to you.*" Jeremiah 30:2. God had a plan for the restoration of Israel and Judah from captivity and delivering them to the land that was promised to their forefathers. God saw it important for Jeremiah to write down those words. For that reason, the promise written came to pass eventually. When we write our plans, visions, and goals, we give them power to manifest in our lives at the appointed time.

Self-confidence

Apart from goal setting and vision inscription, we also need to believe in ourselves and abilities and occasionally shower our own selves with affirmative kind words. You need to remind yourself always that you are good enough no matter any rejection that you may undergo. The impacts of self-affirmation can never be underestimated, especially to young people and its reflection to our general lives.

2

DON'T SETTLE FOR LESS

You are called and chosen for a higher purpose

For many are called, but few are chosen (Matthew 22:14). *But you are a chosen race…* (1 Peter 2:9) *In Him, we were also chosen, having been predestined according to the plan of him who works out everything in conformity with the purpose of His will.* (Ephesians 1:11) This tells us that we have a predefined calling and have been chosen with a purpose according to God's will.

We have been called and chosen in our professions, careers, acts of service and our various capacities for a specific reason of fulfilling our purpose in this world.

You need to understand that you are destined for greatness and that you need to pursue it without compromising your standards.

Hold on to the fight

Life may not be easy even if we are the chosen ones for various tasks in our lives. When God chooses you, He knows that you are capable of doing it, regardless of your vulnerabilities and limitations.

The first disciples were called and chosen when they were fishermen. In that specific time and location, there were probably teachers of law, and other people more educated than them. However their social status did not prevent them from being called into their purpose. Moses in the old testament, was a stammerer , but was still chosen to be the one to deliver the news to Pharaoh, about the plan of rescuing the Israelites from bondage. Through this we learn

Every morning, speak into your own life.

that God recruits, calls and chooses people even at their point of weakness, timidity and imperfections. He knows that you are physically, mentally and spiritually capable of the situation at task.

The problem is that we always want to expect only the good times and not the challenging ones. The fact is that life is made of both. In the Old Testament, the leaders that God called and chose had to undergo the good and the difficult times.

What we need to understand is that God's love is unconditional in our lives no matter how the situation is, even when we can't see the light at the end of the tunnel or when all our hope is gone.

God is unchanging in his love. He loves you. He has a plan for your life. Don't let the newspaper headlines frighten you, because God is still sovereign, He is still on the throne. - Billy Graham

The highs and lows of life are what makes life worth living. If we only had the good times, we wouldn't remember why we were created and whose power we depend upon. When you wake up every morning, always remember that life is a gift, regardless of the troubles, the sorrows, worries or even the huge debts that you may have. Remember that God has chosen you to be alive today. A new day with the gift of life is always a second chance to change everything that you have always wanted to change for the better. Even when today seems so bad in your life, as long as you have hope for tomorrow then, anything can change for the better and for the good of every other thing. Every morning, speak into your own life. Speak powerful words, proclaim and prophecy upon your life. "***Death and life are in the power of the tongue: and they that love it shall eat the fruit thereof.*** (Proverbs 18:21)

Sometimes we worry and stress ourselves so much when God has already set his plans for us and for our benefit. God will provide for us His abundant grace to overcome our worries and fears. We only need to trust Him and let the joy that comes from Him to reign in our hearts.

We have been given power by our heavenly father to be high priests and prophets of our own lives. We have power to speak life into our dreams and aspirations. We have the authority to speak and proclaim good things and blessings to our families and to ourselves. Let us then be aversive to words that can destroy our lives, people's lives and our dreams as well. Focus on the positives in every situation and turn down negative energy in your life. Remember that you are who God says you are. You are a God's child, a daughter or son of a King. *"Yet to all who did receive him, to those who believed in his name, he gave the right to become children of God."* (John 12:12)

Sometimes in life, you will be required to start over from everything you have ever had. It might require every ounce of strength and patience within you. Do not be afraid when this happens, because you are bound to overcome. This time around you will be starting from experience and not from scratch as before.

You are here for a reason. When things become difficult and unbearable with a feeling of giving up, remember that God's plan will always be more beautiful than your disappointments- TobyMac

Remember that you have a reason and a mission outlined, to be fulfilled by you specifically. In all ways and manner, try to guard your heart against all unnecessary turmoil, vengefulness and hatred. *"...for everything you do flows from it."* Proverbs 4: 23

We are required to be the best we can be, to help each other in love and unity without judging each other, because sometimes *"It's not about how much you do, but how much love you put into what you do that counts and when we judge people we have no time to love them. Let us aspire to do the best we can since not all of us can do great things but we can do small things with great love."* - Mother Teresa.

3

GREATER CHALLENGES FOR GREATER RESULTS

Do you have what it takes to make your dream come true?

The fishermen know that the sea is dangerous and the storm terrible, but they have never found those dangers sufficient reasons for remaining ashore. (Vincent van Gogh)

Most people may not be willing to do what it takes to make their dreams come true. Do not be afraid of failing big and dreaming big. You need to have a goal; you need to know your focus in life and where you are heading to. You need to plan, as it is always said, failing to plan is planning to fail. It is also said that to get something that you never had; you must be prepared to do something that you have never done. So, the ultimate take on life is to have both dreams and goals. Both are essential tools for success. Nothing in life is worth having unless we take risks. You might be discouraged in life but no matter what, don't quit without a fight. If you must fall, fall forward. Be grateful for what you have while you are in pursuit of what you exactly want.

There is a story of a girl named Jane*. She was a lovely young girl with a hardworking spirit and a kind heart. She was brought up by her Grandparents in a small village of Mukanda. Jane's mother died during childbirth, while giving birth to her little brother Zack*. They were the only two children of their mother. Their father left them when their mother was four months pregnant with Zack. As Jane* grew older she got to know that her father left, for a journey, never to return. Some of her relatives told her that he now had another family and was living in a village on the other side of the hill. Jane's Grandparents even though elderly, raised their grandchildren with love and good morals.

Jane's grandparents were farmers. They depended on farming as a source of income for their lives and education for their grandchildren. Life was at most times difficult especially when there were seasonal changes such as drought or floods whereby, they would harvest little food which was only enough for them to eat and nothing to take to the market.

Most of the evenings, they would gather around the fireplace and pass time while telling great stories to their grandchildren. They would tell them stories of the times when they were younger and what activities they would do back then. Jane's grandmother would occasionally talk about a woman called Deborah and Jane loved this story.

Deborah was one of the most influential women of her time. She was a prophetess, leader, judge, wife, and mother. During those times, women were looked down upon and could not occupy positions of authority and leadership. However, Deborah defied all odds, by being a leader whom the people of Israel listened to and submitted to her authority. She served her people with strength, honor, and dignity. She was also a noble leader-servant, humble and with authority, who was praised for her leadership. (Judges 4). She was also able to balance her role as judge and her family life as wife and mother. She is an exemplary example and role model of how girls and women should be courageous and confident to serve in various positions of authority without fear and self-criticism.

Jane* would sometimes wonder what would become of her and her brother in the future. She realized that as she grew older, she became more worried about her life. She lacked the motherly love as she dearly missed her late mother, years later after her death. She was also dealing with issues of abandonment, as she always wondered why her father had abandoned them for another family. It was unfortunate that she could only get answers from her mother which was now impossible. She was worried that her grandparents were growing older, and she would soon have to be a parent to her younger brother. In the midst of all this, their occasional lack of school fees didn't make the situation any

Deborah defied all odds, by being a leader whom the people of Israel listened to and submitted to her authority.

better. As a result of all this, Jane*s behavior pattern changed gradually. She was quite a bubbly girl and active in class before, but all that changed. She was now quiet, would want to sit alone during breaktime and withdrew from her friends.

As time passed by, her grandparents were too weak to provide for the family. She had her little brother to take care of and provide emotional support to. Life was not easy and Jane* felt that her world was full of unending problems. Despite all that she remembered her grandmother's words of wisdom, her encouragement and fighting spirit.

Her class teacher, Mrs James noticed the change in her and would occasionally call her after classes for some words of encouragement. She later helped her in filling some sponsorship forms to support her education. She was lucky to win a sponsorship award that catered for her education and that of her brother, up to college. Jane was able to complete her O levels and joined college to pursue a course in Information Technology (IT) and Systems Management. Computers were a new thing to her. In retrospect, the background that she came from in the village, perhaps was the reason why she was so interested to study all about computers and IT.

She later won a scholarship to advance in the same discipline of study in Europe. This was close to a year after her grandparents had passed away due to old age and sickness. Her brother was in the last year of high school and was preparing for his final exams.

Life abroad was quite intriguing. Something she had not experienced before. The infrastructure including the transport system was top notch. She thanked God that a village girl could achieve her dreams despite all the challenges she had faced before. She was excited that all hope was not lost. However, they were still challenges faced abroad. She had to adapt to the cold and rainy winter and inadequate amount of sunshine. The language and accent were quite different and communication with others became a challenge in the first months.

The food and culture were completely different, she had to adapt to all that. In spite of it all, she was determined to achieve the best out of the experience and to be an example to other young girls and boys. This demonstrated that despite what they could go through in life, they could achieve anything they wanted to.

Jane realized that she was struggling with some issues and had to work on herself. It took long before she noticed that her past experiences affected how she formed relationships with others. The gap left by their parents and the suffering she went through had affected her. She sought counsel from therapists, which became of much help to her and family later in life. She went back home after her studies and formed a pioneer startup that now supports the youth in developing their best ideas into fundable projects with the use of Information Technology. She uses her free time to mentor and support the youth in various activities such as sports, guidance, and counselling.

In her story important issues are depicted.

Childhood trauma may be caused by different experiences in a child's life that may portray pain or distress, whether physically or emotionally. These experiences may affect the behaviour of a child, during childhood and may be extended into their adulthood. It is important to seek professional help, counsel, and treatment. It is also equally important to teach our children and teenagers to be open and speak about the problems they are facing in their daily lives. This will save them from falling into negative behaviours such as drug and substance abuse and various addictions as a mechanism of coping with their childhood trauma.

Maternal health care is an important issue that cannot be overemphasized. This refers to health care given to women during pregnancy, childbirth, and the post-natal duration. It is important for countries to put to up systems that protect this vulnerable group of people to prevent losses, pain and death of loved ones.

Abandonment /Rejection

Sometimes in life, we may feel abandoned and alone arising from losing important people in our lives, as a result of death or some kind of separation. We need to understand that time heals our sorrows and that things really get better with time. We need to be hopeful for better days to come. Let it not be a setback towards working on the vision we have of our lives to come.

Diligence

Jane* showed diligence in her work and support towards her family despite the challenges she had. Her consistent efforts earned support towards funding her education and that of her brother. It is important to be consistent on working towards our vision even when we cannot see the light at the end of the tunnel. Light surely comes when we have tried enough and still won't give up!

The greatest glory in living life is not in never falling, but in rising every time we fall. It always seems impossible until it is done. *"A winner is a dreamer who never gives up"*. (Nelson Mandela)

Self-discipline and consistency

This is another important ingredient in this success story. Discipline involves training yourself to do something even when it feels uncomfortable or when you do not want to do it. It takes discipline to actually do what is beneficial for you. In the process, you become uneasy and edgy, and also thrown out of your comfort zone.

Consistency involves maintaining regularity and steadiness in your actions, behavior or tasks that you have set yourself to doing. We may find it difficult to stay on course and focus on goals, projects and plans when there is so much going on around. We want to be more comfortable relaxing on the coach rather than waking up and working towards our dreams. We forget that working on something consistently is key to achieving what we really want in our lives.

There is the law of delayed gratification which when applied in our daily lives goes a long way in helping us achieve what we really want from life. This law proposes a process of foregoing the desire to reward ourselves immediately for the sake of greater future benefits. It involves denying yourself comfort, time or valuables for the purpose of gaining much more benefits in the future. However, in reality, it sometimes becomes difficult to do that daily and consistently, without a conscious decision to undertake this process. An example of this delayed gratification is staying late working on your projects or studies to earn yourselves good grades or finishing up your projects in good time, rather than enjoying a good rest or long hours of sleep. It can also include choosing to eat healthy food and working out rather than having the pleasure of eating addictive and sweet junk food and relaxing on the coach after that. Sacrificing instant benefits will earn greater delayed benefits, which in most cases is required, for you to achieve your dreams and goals in life. *"The place where your greatest discomfort lies is also the spot where your largest opportunity lives."* - Robin Sharma

Self-discipline is important for our growth. It is a component of self-love, because when we are committed to loving ourselves, we are also committed to doing the best we can, for our growth, personal development, and success.

Changing mindset

There is an analogy of iron that states that nothing else can destroy the iron metal except its own rust. In the same way nothing else can destroy a person, apart from his or her mindset. We should therefore, take care of our minds, which have the ability to build us or destroy us if not well taken care of.

There is a story of a man who had a donkey, which had been useful to him for many years. When it was old and tired, the man decided to get rid of it. One day he was going back home together with his donkey, after running the errands of the day. He passed by a deep pit on the ground. He thought that that would be a good chance to get rid of his donkey without necessarily having to kill it. He threw the donkey inside the hole and started covering it with layers of soil. He wanted to bury the donkey alive. His friends passed by and offered to help in burying the donkey. However, one interesting thing was happening inside the hole, which the man and his friends were unaware of. As they were busy heaping the layers and layers of soil into the hole, the donkey kept jumping up layer after layer and consequently getting closer to the exit of the hole. By the time they had finished throwing the layers of soil into the hole, their donkey was able to jump out of the hole. Seeing this, the man was ashamed of himself for doing such a futile job. He gave the donkey to one of his friends and went home. In the end, the donkey's life was saved.

There are so many times in our lives that life throws at us layers and layers of challenges, difficulties, adversities, thoughts of impossibilities, a lot of despair, heartache, and pain. The teaching is that we should rise up from all these layers of challenges in the same way the donkey rose and was finally able to jump out of the pit of death and its life was saved in the end.

Sometimes we go through difficult times in order to believe in ourselves. We can never understand clearly the plan of God in our lives. Suffering will always bring us close to God so that we can acknowledge his ownership of our lives.

If you lose heart in the time of suffering, your strength will depart from you. (Proverbs 24:10)

We are then required to remain steadfast in the times of adversity, lest we lose the strength to continue soldiering on. We may also lose faith in life, which should not be the case.

The challenges in our lives are there to strengthen our convictions. They are not there to run us over! (Nick Vujicic)

Have a picture in mind of a baby learning how to walk, which remains one of the most amazing things to observe in life... the baby puts a step forward, little by little ignorant of where the next step would lead to. The baby is not even sure whether the step would lead to stability or falling onto the ground. Nevertheless he/she is still determined to keep moving until it learns the tricks of keeping itself afloat. Then, there are times when the mother plays with her toddler, throwing it into the air and then catching it just in time at arms' length. At first, the toddler is scared and worried but as the game progresses, the toddler becomes happy and enjoys the game, because it has gained confidence in the mother believing that she cannot let it fall onto the ground.

Sometimes in life, we may not be 100% sure whether the next step we take will lead to our rise or downfall. Then, just like the toddler in the illustration above, we begin to worry and get filled with so much anxiety. If we put our trust in God, no matter how much turbulence and difficulties that we are going through, we are assured that God will hold us at arms-length just like the baby with its mother, and He will not let us fall onto the ground to be destroyed.

When things go wrong, as they sometimes will,
when the road you're trudging seems all uphill,
When the funds are low and the debts are high,
And you want to smile, but you have to sigh,
When care is pressing you down a bit,
Rest if you must, but don't you quit.
Life is strange with its twists and turns,
As every one of us sometimes learns…
Don't give up though the pace seems slow,
You may succeed with another blow.
Success is failure turned inside out,
The silver tint of the clouds of doubt ,
And you never can tell just how close you are,
It may be near when it seems so far,
So stick to the fight when you're hardest hit,
It's when things seem worst that you must not quit,
For all the sad words of tongue or pen,
The saddest are these: "It might have been"

By John Greanleaf Whittier who was an advocate and activist and advocated for the abolition of slavery in the United States.

The most beautiful people are those who have known defeat, known suffering, known struggle, known loss, and have found their way out of the depths. These persons have an appreciation, a sensitivity and an understanding of life that fills them with compassion, gentleness and a deep loving concern. Beautiful people do not just happen." – C.S Lewis

If we want to achieve something different, we must also be prepared to do something extraordinary. We must set our minds in doing what other people have not done or never done before. This is the only way to achieve extraordinary results and attain success.

"If you want something different you must be willing to do something that you have never done" - Thomas Jefferson who was the 3rd President of the USA (1801-1809)

4

LET YOUR LIGHT SHINE

Do not hide your Lamp under the table

No one lights a lamp and then puts it under a basket, instead a lamp is placed on a stand where it gives light to everyone in the house. (Matthew 5:15-16)

Let your light shine before others, so that they may see your good works and give glory to your Father who is in heaven.

And as we let our own light shine, we unconsciously give other people permission to do the same. (Nelson Mandela)

Dimming someone else's light won't make yours shine any brighter - Rebel Dietitian.

In the same way, dimming your own light won't make anyone else's shine any brighter. The only thing that might happen is that it will deprive of the world greatest talents and abilities as a result of our lack of being brave enough to embrace and believe in our authentic abilities. There are times when we doubt ourselves frequently asking ourselves questions like, Am I good enough? Am I fit to do this job or to carry out particular tasks that have been assigned to me? Am I good enough to be a leader? Will the people like me?

Most of the time, we find ourselves overshadowed by the cloud of self-criticism. In addition to self-criticism –

> *The universe needs your time, your efforts, gifts and treasures.*

which is very detrimental to our lives - we might also have the fear of external or societal criticism. This is the fear of what people will say or do to us when, we do certain things that show our abilities and talents in the limelight. As a result, we tend to cave in and withdraw from people, situations or even ceremonies. In doing this, we dim our own light and prevent it from shining. Consequently, we succeed in hiding our abilities, talents and goodness from other people, which could be helpful to our communities, societies, the country and even the world at large.

I was a culprit of hiding my lamp under the table. I would shy off and hide my abilities, talents and knowledge from people so that I couldn't attract unnecessary attention. In the end, this could be harmful because we are not able to stretch and explore our talents and God-given abilities for His greater glory.

The world needs the talent that you have. The universe needs your time, your efforts, gifts and treasures.

What are you doing with what you have? You may not have much money in your hands or pockets, but you may have gifts, talents and skills on your hands. Do not fear failure. If you don't fail, you are not even trying. You have to take chances in your life as long as it is for a good cause.

I like a quote by Les Brown who said that, ***the graveyard is the richest place on earth, because it is here where you will find all the hopes and dreams, (talents and abilities that were never fulfilled or utilized)… (following emphasis by author), the books that were never written, the songs that were never sung, the inventions that were never shared, the cures that were never discovered, all because someone was too afraid to take that first step, keep with the problem, or determined to carry out their dream.*** We must use what we've got before it is too late.

You might not necessarily be defined by what possessions you have, but by what you have got inside of you, your character, motivation and the faith that you have within you.

There is no passion to be found by playing small. - **In settling for a *life that is less than the one that you are capable of living* -** Nelson Mandela.

Let us therefore use our talents for the good of our communities, societies and the world at large. God wants us to honour Him with the gifts, talents and abilities that he has given us.

Do not only aspire to make a living, aspire to make a difference - Denzel Washington.

> *We are all different from each other, created in likeness of God and with different abilities.*

In whatever thing you are good at no matter how "small" it may appear to be, use it to honour God and he will bless you abundantly and with more than what you expected from Him. It might be singing, creative art, paintings, cooking, IT skills, leadership or service in whatever capacity. We are all different from each other, created in likeness of God and with different abilities. That is why we need each other because we were created to co-exist and depend on each other.

He who began a good work in you will perfect it until the day of Christ Jesus. Philippians 1:6 God has purposed for us to use our unique roles and abilities to serve others as faithful stewards and leaders, to bless others and to glorify and honour Him who is the source of all these gifts. In whatever we do, in our activities, let us perfect them as if we are doing for God who is the giver of life who will bless us abundantly. "***Whatever you do, work heartily, as for the Lord and not for men, knowing that from the Lord you will receive inheritance as your reward. You are serving the Lord Christ***". Col 3:23-24

Using our talents and abilities to seek justice and fight against oppression on people is honourable. Using our position in society to correct and fight against discrimination is even more admirable.

Marilyn Monroe was a famous American star - an actress, who also owned a film production company and won a Golden Globe for the best actress in 1959. Marilyn had her downfalls too since she faced personal difficulties, anxiety and a tainted image towards the end of her career before finally meeting her death.

However, Marilyn Monroe, being white in race, used her talent to prevent the oppression of the minority racial groups in America during her time. Marilyn was a good friend and a fan of a top famous Jazz Singer Ella Fitzgerald, who was the first African American woman in History to win the Grammy Awards. However, this was not all rosy from the beginning. Ella was denied so many chances to perform, in auditions and events, only because she was a woman of colour. She faced a lot of racial discrimination at the debut of building her career. Marilyn on the other hand at the time was already a star; she had already made a name for herself. It was easier for white people to succeed in their careers than those of African American origin. Marilyn and Ella were good friends and had a lot in common including their difficult childhoods. Marilyn used her fame to help Ella grow her music career as a Jazz singer. She would sit at the front row in events and bring other celebrities in, if only they allowed Ella, the black woman, to sing at these events. She really showed great support for her friend Ella and aided her in battling prejudice because of her skin colour. As a result, Ella became a force to reckon with, a woman who made history as the first black woman to win a Grammy award. This is a good example of how we can use our talents, or position in society to uphold the good and promote social justice.

"When we dim our own light, it doesn't make anyone else's shine brighter. It just deprives the world of what we could have offered it if we had been brave enough to fully embody our authentic selves" - Rebel Dietitian.

5

SERVING OTHERS YIELDS PURPOSE

We find our purpose through serving others

Children learn faster by emulation. They emulate what they see people do. It is actually difficult to make them do something that they haven't seen being done before. To be good instructors and teachers of good service and commendable leadership to humanity, we must be prepared to act as good examples. Our intentions should always reflect our actions. The question that we can ask ourselves for a purposeful life is how we can be of service to others - how we can be an instrument of love, courage, compassion and kindness to others. Service to others gives us a fulfillment, satisfaction and creates a bond through connection with others.

The world is changed by your example, not by your opinion. - Paulo Coelho

Focusing on ourselves will never reveal our life's purpose. (Rick Warren)

Leadership is best demonstrated as acts of service to others.

Leadership is best demonstrated as acts of service to others.

We can borrow some life lessons from the most renowned leaders in the world such as Nelson Mandela, Mahatma Gandhi and Martin Luther King Jr, among many others.

We have to pursue things greater than ourselves. Most people admit that if they only thought about themselves they would not care about what they would want to change in other peoples' lives and the society in general. Most of the renowned leaders that brought change to their societies and countries did not care about themselves entirely. They had a heart that cared for their people, which gave them a purpose of service and leadership to change the lives and living conditions of their people.

"A life of significance is about serving those who need your gifts, your leadership, your purpose - Kevin Hall"

"If you want to lift yourself up, lift up someone else." The world cares very little about what a man or a woman knows, it is what a man or woman is able to do that counts. (Booker T. Washington)

"As we lose ourselves in the service of others we discover our own lives and our own happiness." - Dieter F. Uchtdorf

This takes me to the story of a teacher and priest from Kenya, Peter Tabichi who was crowned to be the best in the world after winning the 2019 Global teacher Prize of US $1million. He is a good example of finding purpose in the service of others. Before winning the prize, he had been working as a dedicated teacher at a rural secondary school. That school is located in a semi-arid area and an impoverished region in Kenya. Teaching in such a school with dedication and a heart of service will most times prove to have many challenges in his life and the daily lives of the students taught by him. His colleagues confirmed that he was a dedicated, hardworking, humble and kind teacher.

Apart from teaching, he also dedicated his service to advocate for the rights of the less privileged and children. He also advocated for the inclusivity of girls to be educated (for rural communities that looked down on girls, not allowing them to go to school). The Varkey Foundation reported that he had changed the lives of his students in many ways, including the introduction of science clubs and the promotion of peace between different ethnic groups and religions. He also worked on improving the self-esteem and confidence of his students through nurturing their abilities and talents using music, robotics, science and technology. It had never occurred in his life that people would recognise his efforts after he was awarded this great prize, by the Varkey Foundation in Dubai, UAE in March 2019. In the end, no matter how hard and challenging it may be, our service to others gives us purpose in life.

"The life's most persistent and urgent question is: What are you doing for others?" - Martin Luther King

The late Wangari Maathai was the 2004 Nobel peace prize winner. She had dedicated her life to the service of others, and through her dedication to work in the conservation of Kenya's environment. She found her purpose and pride as the founder of Kenya's Environmental Green Belt Movement. She is remembered to have planted 30 million trees in Kenya and initiated the planting of at least 1 billion trees worldwide. Through the planting of trees in Kenya, she led to the generation of income for 100,000 women in that period. Wangari Maathai surely had a vision and had already figured out her purpose in life, but it was not easy for her. She had to set out to oppose the cutting down of trees with an aim of saving the forests that are important in maintaining favorable climate to prevent aridity, drought, and consequential famine in many parts of Kenya. That was not a walk in the park for her especially when she was faced with so much opposition by the governing leaders and political regime of her time. She faced death in so many instances as her life was occasionally threatened. In all that, she did not give up on her dream and purpose of having a better country that respects and cares for plants, trees and the environment at large. Today, she is remembered for the sacrifice, determination, dedication and the courage that she had towards this quest, which has surely changed the lives of people she left behind for the better.

In the course of History, there comes a time when humanity is called to shift to a new level of consciousness, to reach a higher moral ground, a time when we have to shed our fear and give hope to each other; that time is now. - Wangari Mathaai

There is the story of the late Chadwick Boseman, who will always be remembered as a true legend and a superhero in many films that changed the history of the entertainment industry especially for the black community worldwide. He showed kids of African descent that superheroes can also look like them. A situation that did not exist before. He starred in close to six life-changing films that truly made a positive and life changing impact in many people both young and old, from all races and generations. He quickly became a role model to many actors in the Entertainment world. He came to change the stereotypical thoughts about black people in America, first by becoming a figure of young talented and black actors with good principles and values that people around the world could emulate. Sadly, that did not come easy for him even though he had an intrinsic drive that no one could turn down. In the beginning of his acting career, he was given roles that did not suit his purpose - roles that portrayed his people and race negatively, portraying bad moral values and negative behaviour. He was supported very well in that particular role but he soon realised that it was not his place. He wanted to change lives and influence people in a positive way. After asking questions on his acting role, which did not portray good values about people of his race, he was fired from his job. Despite that, he did not give up. He still had a vision for his purpose. God was not yet done with him.

> *The struggles along the way are only meant to shape you for your purpose.*

The struggles along the way are only meant to shape you for your purpose - Chadwick Boseman.

During the last four years of his career before his death, Chadwick Boseman had dedicated himself to change the lives of people who watched his films. Particularly, the famous movie "the black panther" took the world by storm, showing the greatness of the African soil, culture and most of all, that they could become anything they wanted in life, if they put work and passion into what they do. He fulfilled his purpose in those last four years of his life. Sadly, at the same time he had been secretly battling with colon cancer. In between all the surgeries and chemotherapy sessions that he went through while fighting the disease, he still appeared for rehearsals, film practice and still mastered martial arts in preparation of the filming of all the movies he featured. During that time when he was sick, it is when he featured in the greatest of all movies, the "***Black panther.* 'Your greatest ministry will most likely come out of your greatest hurt.'** - Rick Warren "

This phrase has come to pass in the lives of many people who have positively impacted other people's lives and proclaimed their greatest testimonies after going through their greatest periods of hardships, great hurt and pain.

Up to date, I'm still awed by the passion and determination that Chadwick had for his purpose and career. He really made a difference through making people believe and have courage in themselves, especially among the black community in America and the world at large.

6

CHALLENGES ARE INEVITABLE

Hope for good; prepare for the worst

This takes me back to the tragic airplane accident that happened in Ethiopia in April 2019 that killed 159 passengers on board. Majority were Kenyans, including many other nationals that were on board in that particular plane. The only questions that were left in people's minds were: Why did it happen? Why so tragic? Couldn't God have stopped it because he knew it would happen anyway?

There is also the story of a man who got to the airport late for that particular flight and the airport attendants barred him from boarding the plane. He kept cursing and shouting for a long time, while he was booked onto the next flight. As soon as he learnt about the plane crash and that he could have been in that tragic accident, he could not stop thanking God for saving his life. The mystery is that someone's life was saved as a misfortune of missing his flight while other lives were lost for being in the right place and time. This takes us back to realise that our lives are not our own. In whatever we do, God's will has to happen. We make our plans but God establishes. (Proverbs 16:1)

God's mercies are new every morning. Lam 3:23

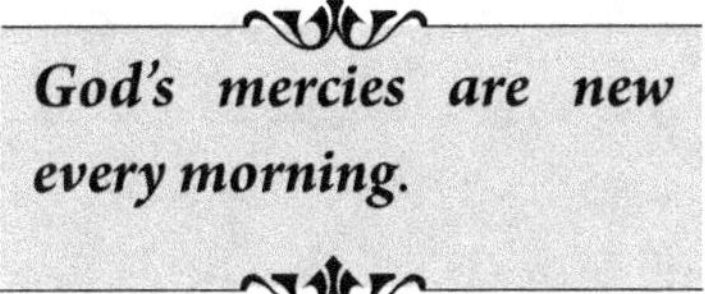

This teaches us that we will always make our plans but they have to be in line with God's will for us in order for them to work successfully. Father, if you are willing, remove this cup from me. Yet not my will, but Yours be done. (Luke 22:42) Jesus who is God's son also had to submit himself to the will of His father. He endured so much pain and suffering from the hands of mere men who were inferior to him, humbling himself and accepting to die yet he was immortal. This was only for one reason - for God's will to be done. I have attended various retreats where in one occasion I heard a person who testified how he had tried all kinds of businesses. He had injected a lot of capital but all of them failed. One day, he decided to seek God's will and the business that he started thereafter flourished in a thousand-fold. This therefore enables us to understand that in everything we do, we should always ask God if it is in accordance with His will.

People asked Jesus if the blind man's blindness was caused by his own sins or those of his parents? (John 9:3). Jesus answered them that it was not because of their sins; this happened so that the works of God would be manifested in him.

"Being in prison gave me purpose"

This is a life experience of a Kenyan woman Teresia Njoroge. The circumstances under which she found herself in Jail were unfathomable.

Teresia Njoroge previously worked for a bank until one time she was framed for theft and conspiracy to defraud the bank that she worked at. That is how she ended up in prison – a case that up to today, her stand remains that she was innocent. The court case went on for some time until in 2009, the judge passed on the judgement of her imprisonment. She describes it as a day that she felt as if her world came crashing down before her feet. She ended up in prison from 2009-2011 together with her infant baby who was just months old. She lost a lot of friends and other people who didn't want to associate themselves with a "**thief**". She weaned her baby while in prison and life moved on.

While in the prison, she talked to other female inmates to learn about their stories and their reasons for their imprisonment. She discovered that most of their reasons were very minor cases but they had been behind bars for many years. Some were still in prison because they lacked as little as Ksh. 2000 to bail themselves out of prison. Teresia was saddened by that state of affairs. She was filled with pity for these women. She felt luckier even though she was in the same situation with them. Some women also had children there in jail but their situations were worse than Teresia's. She was lucky that her family would visit her often and they would bring with them the necessities that her child needed. On the contrary some women with their children had never seen a family member come to visit them in a very long time, leave alone bringing necessities for them. Teresia found herself in a situation where she could ask her family to bring extra necessities for her baby so that she could share with other mothers, for their children in prison.

She started teaching other women in prison who were illiterate. She taught them how to read and write, basic accounting skills, making budgets, saving money and business proposal writing - a credit to her previous career, working in the bank. Some women, she described in prison were in despair. Loneliness and regret was written all over their faces without hope of the unfortunate situation ever coming to an end.

In 2011, Teresia managed to get out of prison. The problem was that a lot had happened and could not be undone. She faced a lot of stigma though her family supported her. Later, she was vindicated of the crime she had not committed. The court revealed that it had been a wrong conviction! She had suffered a lot yet she was innocent. She says that being in prison gave her purpose. After prison, she started visiting churches and women groups to voice out the challenges that women are facing in prison and this led to her forming programmes that look after the needs of women in Kenyan prisons and also helping them start life afresh by offering them self-employment opportunities, capital and empowerment. Teresia had seen the plights of women and girls in prison amidst poverty, rejection, stigma crime and lack of opportunities. She created a path of change and purpose by founding the Clean Start Solutions Kenya. This is an organisation with a focus and mission of equipping, empowering, and preparation of imprisoned women and girls for the uncertain journey of their integration back into the society. She has received various awards in Kenya for a really good job that she is doing. From her terrible experience in prison, Teresia found a greater purpose in life - standing up for the rights and needs of women in and after imprisonment. This is something that she could not have started if she was still working in the bank. Now she has a bigger dream of helping the community and society in general. Pain and suffering gave her a purpose to live for.

> *"Success is to be measured not by the position that one has reached in life, but by the obstacles which s/he has overcome."*

An American educator and author, Booker T. Washington once said, *"Success is to be measured not by the position that one has reached in life, but by the obstacles which s/he has overcome."*

"Comfort and prosperity have never enriched the world as much as adversity has. God never takes something from your life without replacing it with something better". –Billy Graham

Blow to the world

At the end of the year 2019 going forward to the new decade 2020, there was an outbreak of a disease, which turned out to be a major pandemic. The world had never experienced it before. (However, other pandemics of different types had been experienced before).

The disease that would come to be known as COVID-19 (Coronavirus Disease - 2019) originated from Wuhan, China. It later spread to all continents in the world leading to 1.5 million confirmed deaths and 64 million confirmed cases of coronavirus infections worldwide by the end of March 2021.

This led to a declaration of Emergency situation by the World Health Organization. The WHO proposed strict quarantine measures of people at homes and lockdown in major cities of the world as a result of controlling the rate of spreading of the virus. Many countries especially in Africa organised and held National days of prayer, turning to God to pardon and help them during the pandemic.

Go home, my people, and lock your doors! Hide yourselves for a little while until the Lord's anger has passed. Look, The Lord is coming from heaven to punish the people of the earth for their sins. The earth will no longer hide those who have been killed. They will be brought out for all to see. (Isaiah 26:20-21)

Many people believed that it was a punishment and wrath from God for the crimes, injustices, murder, corruption and selfishness of political leaders among many wrong doings in the society and the world at large. People cried to God to forgive them their sins and intervene for them in that situation as it is written in 2 Chronicles 7:13-15.

Whenever I hold back the rain or send locusts to eat up the crops or send an epidemic on my people if they pray to me and repent and turn away from the evil they have been doing, then I will hear them in heaven, forgive their sins, and make their land prosperous again. I will watch over this temple and be ready to hear all the prayers that are offered here.

Cast your care unto the Lord and he will sustain you. Psalm 55:22

In the year progressing on to 2021, the pandemic of the Covid-19 led to the shutdown of economic progress of countries as a result of lock down in most countries of the world. Tough times were experienced for both the rich and the poor. It was a difficult moment that lasted a period of more than a year. It was a period of suffering for most countries in the world; a time when there was a recorded highest increase in economic recession. Many people died of that virus. This resulted to an almost repeat of the Spanish flu pandemic (1918-1919) that affected the whole world and resulted to high mortality rates of about 50 million people especially the age group between 20- 40-years. The measures of this pandemic involved the maintenance of practices such as good personal hygiene, isolation, quarantine, use of disinfectants and limitations of public gatherings. People were locked up in their houses for months. The towns as well as cities were also shut down.

Cast your care unto the Lord and he will sustain you.

With all that suffering, could there be something positive to derive from this situation. In my mind, I thought that no matter how difficult the situation was, this could lead to healing and restoration of the earth. People would change their perspectives towards life. They would change their thoughts to give priority to things that had value and those that really matter in life. They would give more importance to their lives and families because in the end, that was what mattered most during the pandemic. They would give more importance to professions such as doctors, nurses, medics and teachers who mattered most and who were at the front line battling the pandemic. Families would begin to heal, since there would be more time spent in the family units rather than behind a desk at work or outside on trips.

And people stayed at home
And read books
And listened
And they rested
And did exercises
And made art and played
And learned new ways of being
And stopped and listened
More deeply
Someone meditated, someone prayed
Someone met their shadow,
And people began to think differently
And people healed.
And in the absence of people who
 Lived in ignorant ways
Dangerous, meaningless and heartless,
The earth also began to heal
And when danger ended and
People found themselves
They grieved for the dead
And made new choices
And dreamed of new visions
And created new ways of living
And completely healed the earth
Just as they were healed
Poem written in 1869 by Kathleen O'Mara

Reprinted during the Spanish flu pandemic 1918- 1919.

7

PRICE FOR PURPOSE

"There is no victory without a battle, no testimony without a test, and no miracle without an impossible circumstance." - Kris Vallotton

At some point in life, we may not get the comfortable life that we hoped for - a comfortable life full of peace, love from everybody, fame and a lot of wealth. Most of the great people have had very difficult times in pursuit of their purpose. Most world leaders have suffered greatly, for long periods. Sometimes, the greater part of their lives have been filled with suffering and pain, while in the pursuit of freedom, battles against social injustices, discrimination, among other important issues in society. This includes renown world leaders such as Martin Luther King and Nelson Mandela, who have been examples of leaders that have suffered oppression while in the pursuit of a revolution.

The first presidents of most countries in Africa endured life in prison for years while in their pursuit of bringing freedom and independence to their countries. That was their purpose, which they paid through their own dear lives.

The first president of the Republic of Kenya, Mzee Jomo Kenyatta played a significant role in the transformation of his country, Kenya from the British colony into an independent republic. He was among the group of young able men who were also known as the "the freedom fighters" or the "MAUMAU". This was a group that fought against colonialism in the 1950s in Kenya. He was imprisoned for close to 10 years and after he was released, he became part of a political party, KANU that led the country into its independence. This is what Jomo Kenyatta, among other freedom fighters had to pay as a cost for the independence of the republic of Kenya.

The late Nelson Mandela was a good example of selfless leaders that sacrificed their whole youthful life for the independence and freedom of the people of South Africa. He won the Nobel peace prize in 1993 jointly with F.W de Klerk for the contribution towards the peaceful termination of the segregation and one of the worst times in the history of South Africa during the apartheid regime. This is illustrated in Mandela's autobiography, the "**Long Walk to Freedom**".

Mandela had great political courage to fight for the change of the lives of his people, no matter what it would cost him. That was during the apartheid regime that was filled with ethnic disparities, racially conditioned suppression and a lot of discrimination in addition to colonialism. He formed a party that would fight for

_______________________ the freedom and rights of his

people, the African National Congress (ANC). Being the party's leader, he was sentenced to life imprisonment, which later became 28 years of prison life. In his book, the "**Long walk to Freedom**", Mandela describes his jail sentence of 28 years of imprisonment. These years were marked with excessive cruelty by prison guards, backbreaking labour, poor living conditions of suffering and inhabitable miniscule cells. After all what he went through, he was later released from prison and the struggle continued for the independence of his country leading to victory when he became the president of South Africa. *"Do not judge me for my success, judge me for how many times I fell down and got back up again"*- Nelson Mandela.

It is also unfortunate that sometimes people in general are still resistant to change on issues that people had already fought against and died for, for instance the unjust killings and racial discrimination. So many years after leaders that fought against oppression of black people in North America, Africa and around the globe, it is sad to note that these issues still happen in society and many people still lose their lives through such social injustices. On May, 25th 2020 in Minneapolis, Minnesota, there was killing of an innocent black man, George Floyd by white police men triggered by racial discrimination. This led to worldwide demonstrations and protests against the use of excessive force by police, lack of police accountability, and police racism and discrimination. The late Martin Luther King and his counterparts had suffered a lot in their lives towards the fighting for the rights of the black race in America, which continues to trend with the slogan "**Black lives matter**".

Excessive force by police and unjust homicides by citizens still continue to take place in many countries in the world including my native country, Kenya. This is long after people have held demonstrations about these crimes and many have lost their lives and property while in the pursuit of justice for their loved ones and family members.

Martin Luther King experienced a fair share of suffering in his quest toward a revolution against racial discrimination in America. He became the first president of the Southern Christian Leadership Conference. (SCLC). He won the Nobel peace prize in 1964 for his contribution towards the struggle against violence and racial discrimination in America.

He dreamt of a day when all inhabitants of the United States, would be judged by their personal qualities and not by the colour of their skin. "**I have a dream that one day, this nation will rise up and live out the true meaning of its creed. We hold these truths to be self - evident that all men are created equal**" - Martin Luther King. He was later assassinated for the same struggle he fought for, which was the price he paid for his dream.

The prices people pay in pursuit of a purpose are usually painful and might not even end well. This requires a selfless mindset, commitment and most certainly the most important virtue in this quest, which is sacrifice.

Seeking justice and fighting against oppression on people is honourable. Using our position in the society to correct and fight against discrimination is even more admirable "**Learn to do good, seek justice, correct oppression, bring justice to the fatherless, and plead the widow's caus**e." Isaiah 1:17

Similarly, in our lives there are prices we have to pay in pursuit of purpose. We may lose friends who were dear to us. We may lack enough time with our families. Some have even lost their jobs and sources of livelihood while in this quest. Let us not have the fear of criticism. Yes, people will judge us; some will criticize us when we go for what we believe in, with the aim of making a difference and influencing positive change in people's lives. Sometimes in life, we may find ourselves in a situation where some friends will be friendly to us only when we are at the same level and at par with each other. On the other hand, once we get to the top or climb up at the ladder we may get judged and criticized. When this happens, remember it's lonely at the top and you will have to stand your ground, because if you don't get things done, no one will.

Remember too, that life is a journey with it twists and turns. You might start life's journey with people , and along the way you may add some to into your life, in the same way, you might lose others too. That must happen for your journey to be complete.

We should always remember that the power of the purpose must be greater than the pain we experience along the journey. - Billy Cox

I like the encouraging story of a renowned Christian Leader

TD Jakes, on the challenges and triumphs of building up his ministry. At some point, he went through so many challenges, that he almost quit. Many were the times, when people opposed him before they even knew him or what value he offered. Many were the times when people opposed his ministry even before they knew what it was all about. He eventually became shattered, discouraged and fell into despair. It had to take the testimony of a young woman who he hadn't met before to turn his life around. This woman attested that she was almost dying in hospital when her baby died in her womb and she was severely sick, but the preachings of TD Jakes that she kept listening repeatedly to, are what kept her alive and gave her new hope to live, every single day while she was bedridden in hospital. After hearing the testimony of that young woman, TD Jakes who had already thrown in the towel, rose up, withdrew from his sadness and stood to his feet to give the ministry a fresh start. He finally realized that his work was already in God's hands and surrendered to God to direct his path. His work began to flourish from then onwards.

Do not give up on your purpose; it will not always be easy.

When you are genuinely devoted to God, call upon him in the days of trouble, He will rescue you, so that you can glorify Him. Psalm 50:15

Do not give up on your purpose; it will not always be easy. Purposeful lives are achieved through struggles, but what keeps us focused to the goal is the result or achievement in the end, no matter how long it may take. *"If you feel like you are losing everything, remember that trees lose all their leaves every year and they still stand tall and wait for better days to come"* - Subham Kumar Mal

8

MAKING GOOD JUDGEMENT AND DECISIONS

Many are the situations in which we are faced with tasks of making the right choices in our lives. We tend to fear the consequences of failure in case we make the wrong choices. This could be financial, career-wise or even in looking for a life partner. There will be times when we won't know the right path to take in our lives. There will be times that we think that we have made the right decision only to be disappointed in the end, which would mean that we didn't make the right choice. There are other times that we may wait for God to grant us the desires of our hearts, but then again we think that we have waited for too long, according to our human mindsets.

In all these, we need to involve our creator, our maker to give us wisdom in whatever we do. He gives us whatever we need in our lives according to His perfect will and time. *"But seek first the kingdom of God, and his righteousness, and all these things shall be added unto you"*. Mat 6:33 He knows what we need; our work is to seek Him and all things desired in good faith will be granted unto us. I remember God saving me so many times from dangerous situations and from what I would call *"the hands of the enemy."* During one particular time, I didn't know that I was in a dangerous situation because everything in my eyes seemed normal to me. On the contrary I really needed God's protection, which I didn't even ask for, at that particular moment, because everything appeared just right for me. Reflecting back on the events that followed thereafter, I realised that God really saved me, when I thought that I was safe. I realised that God knew exactly what I needed for that particular moment, even when I was unaware of it and hadn't prayed about it. This is what happens to us sometimes, when we take a particular direction in life and become so stubborn insisting on taking a particular route. On the contrary, God may be redirecting us to another route because he is trying to protect us from danger that we know nothing about. However, sometimes we become stubborn and don't want to listen to God's direction and voice. We end up taking our route, unguided that leads to regrets. *"But my people would not listen to me, Israel would not submit to me, So I gave them over to their own stubborn hearts to follow their own devices"*. Psalm 81:11-12.

This is a reminder about several times in the history of Israel when the people didn't listen to God's voice and message that was addressed to them through the prophets. The kings together with the people became stubborn over time and would not listen to God's messengers. This ended up to their nation's destruction and captivity. God gave them up to their knowledge, and counsel and this path led to their destruction. The wisdom of humankind is foolishness to God. We need God's wisdom to guide us in our lives. As humans we rely on Him who has spiritual eyes to see what is unseen by humankind. He sees our souls, the intentions of our hearts, our thoughts and even our spirits.

How do we listen to God's voice? How do we ask for God's wisdom, and eyes of discernment that cannot be fathomed by normal eyes of humankind? How should we know from God the path that He wants us to take?

A Motivational speaker, Jim Rohn, said, "*We are the average of the five people we spend the most time with.*" This relates to the law of averages, which is the theory that indicates, the result of any given situation will be the average of all outcomes.

> "*We are the average of the five people we spend the most time with.*"

We are witnesses that we pick habits from our friends, relatives and family that we spend most of the time with. We become an average of their habits by the law of averages depicted above. In the same way, if we desire to act, think and have wisdom of God, we need to spend more time with Him. How do we achieve this? We need to spend time reading God's word, to pray and worship Him often. We need to invite Him in our lives to be our friend as much as He is our father. Spending our time with Him in this way will enable us to hear His voice and act like him. With time, we are granted His wisdom that makes us rule our lives according to His will.

In life, we make choices based on our experiences, knowledge, understanding, wisdom and intuition. Through critical thinking and the tools mentioned. Most of the time we would think that we have made the right choices. In some cases, we would have good decisions but in other instances, we find that we made the wrong choices or decisions. This is because we rely on our own judgments and sometimes our judgements may not be right since they depend on our human selves and experiences, which are bound to make human errors. For these reasons, we need intervention, direction and sound judgement from a superior being that is on a higher level than the human self.

Trust in the Lord with all your heart and do not rely on your own understanding. In all your ways acknowledge Him and he will direct your paths. Prov 3:5-6

Trust in the Lord with all your heart and do not rely on your own understanding.

We are called to ask God to direct our paths always in decision making because we are bound to make mistakes, when we rely on our judgements because of our human nature.

Getting informed and looking for knowledge for better decision making is important. Where there is no guidance the people fall but in an abundance of counselors, there is safety. Prov 11: 14

The motives of the decisions must be pure and not to harm. Do not make hasty decisions, they should be coupled with good reasons, prior knowledge and sober judgement. It is not good for a person to be without knowledge, he who makes haste with his feet errs. Prov 19:2

Sometimes we may not hear God's voice or direction, when we are faced with important decisions to make. Personally, what I have learnt over the years, concerning making the right decision, is that, first, our motives must be right and Godly. Secondly, no matter how difficult the decision-making will be, it must be the choice that gives you peace in your heart, because, **"God is not of disorder or confusion but of peace."** 1 Cor 14:33

Looking up to God gives us sound judgement, intuition, gut instinct, and spiritual discernment. You can listen and get vibrations from within and get a better understanding of the events that occur around you. You may not understand it but your guts and intuition will reveal the truth that you are looking for.

In some instances in life, we can have the capability of discerning prophetic visions of our own lives. This involves having the ability to receive the guidance of the Holy Spirit freely to confirm and or to contradict what we think that we know. The Holy Spirit becomes a helper who teaches us and enables us to have the right conscience. Through this, we are given wisdom over our lives and we are able to receive revelations through the Holy Spirit. As a result, we become better people and we are able to know our creator better. We are granted talents, abilities and spiritual gifts in order to bear good fruits that bring positive change to the world and for the demonstration of God's honour and glory. We are given the hope of salvation, His truths are revealed to us, and we are given more knowledge of his works, of what is yet to come or happen and to receive the true inheritance of the works of Christ." ***But you are a chosen race, a royal priesthood, a holy nation, a people for his own possession, that you may proclaim the excellences of him who called you out of darkness into his marvelous light.*** " 1 Pet. 2:9

9

REJOICING WHILE TRUSTING

Treasure what you have as you focus your faith on God's promises

Patience and perseverance are virtues that we will all need in this journey of life. There is a reward for our patience and perseverance, no matter how long we will wait for that which we long for. In the period of waiting upon the Lord, it is paramount that we give thanks for what we already have. We should not forget to be happy in the present moments that we have in life. Let us not wait to obtain the things that we hope for so that we can start being happy. Let us enjoy the process of becoming who we want to be.

We may assume that life will be complete when we get good

grades, graduate from university, get a high paying job, get material things, get a spouse and a family but sometimes, this does not bring the fulfillment we have been yearning for. After getting what we have always wished for in life, we might experience new challenges that come along with what we had desired most. For instance, we might get frustrated with that job because it might be too demanding, which may make us lack time for family. Once we get the kids that we have always wished for, we might long for the time when the kids will be old enough to be more independent. When the kids are old enough, we then start worrying about handling their teenage years. The truth of the matter is that

> *Try to live each day as if it is the last day of our lives.*

every stage of life will come with its joys, sorrows, challenges, and triumphs. We should therefore be present to experience, to treasure and to enjoy each moment at the beginning, center and end of every stage of our lives.

Share your joys and spend time with your family, and those that value you most. Remember to visit and also help those in need. Time waits for no man and the chance that we have will not last forever. We should therefore, try to live each day as if it is the last day of our lives.

But they that wait upon the Lord shall renew their strength. They shall mount up with wings like eagles, they shall run and not be weary, they shall walk and not faint. (Isaiah 40:31)

A quote from Alfred D. Souza on this perspective that states,

For a long time it had seemed to me that life was about to begin - real life. But there was always some obstacle in the way, something to be gotten through first, some unfinished business, time still to be served, or a debt to be paid. Then life would begin. At last,

> A great blessing needs a prepared vessel.

it dawned on me that these obstacles were my life. As a summary "There is no better time to be happy than right now."

God is capable of providing us with everything we need according to the promises that He has kept for us. He is in control of your every situation no matter how grave the situation might be. Through our sorrows, we are rewarded with greater blessings. If we are capable of getting the best then we should also be prepared for the worst. His grace is always sufficient for us.

Therefore, let us look around and appreciate the simple things in life - they matter too. "Gratitude is the healthiest of all human emotions. The more you express gratitude for what you have, the more likely you get even more to express gratitude for." - Zig Zagler

Be prepared

Preparedness is an important quality that we should have in all aspects of our lives. Preparedness simply means being ready for a forthcoming event, situation or action.

As we prepare for better things to come in our lives, every advancement we make in life will still come with its own challenges.

As we wait for breakthroughs in our lives, we don't need to just sit and wait. We need to go on with our lives. We need to have faith and keep on working to better ourselves each day as we prepare for those great blessings. **A great blessing needs a prepared vessel**. You need to get prepared for that breakthrough that you have always wanted. You will never get prepared by just being idle.

"We hear that some among you are idle and disruptive. They are not busy; they are busybodies. Such people we command and urge in the Lord Jesus Christ to settle down and earn the food they eat." – 2 Thessalonians 3:11-12

Faith

It is during the wait, when we take a big step of faith. To enroll in that programme that you have always wanted. To start that project or business that you have always desired to have. To apply for that job that you always wanted but felt that you were not good enough. To leave toxic situations that you have always feared to get out of. Once you take that big step of faith, you will then be

My message to you is that you live by faith even when you can't see the light at the end of the tunnel.

prepared for a bigger blessing coming your way. My message to you is that you live by faith, taking a first step when you can't see the destination. We may not be required to do great things but indeed take small steps of faith in obedience and He will do wonders. We should live like sons and daughters of a king because our heavenly father is full of wisdom and riches and is capable of catering for our needs. When filled with fear in our lives, let us anchor ourselves in the word of God for nothing is too big or even too small for Him to accomplish for you.

Let us also always remain optimistic in life like Joshua in the bible, who was able to attest triumph where there was no sign of it - to speak victory over our lives even when we can't see our lives' direction and heading. This is a show of faith. Living a purposeful life demands being optimistic in life. It tells us that we take the first step, even when we can't see the whole staircase.
– Martin Luther King Junior

God was happy with the faith that Abraham had in Him. Faith profoundly moves the heart of God. God admired the total faith, complete trust and obedience that Abraham had in Him. Abraham was willing to sacrifice the only son that he got after waiting for so long. That faith was admirable. It is unimaginable that you can wait for more than 50 years to get a baby and when you get it, you are asked to sacrifice it. That is what moved the heart of God.

"In life, you don't get what you want, you get what you believe" – Oprah Winfrey. Then you have to believe in yourself. This might seem as a cliché to many people. However, putting this phrase into action is not always easy; it will take a whole lot of faith to propel you to who or where you have always dreamt to be.

Let us then with confidence approach the throne of grace, that we may receive mercy and find grace to help in time of need. (Hebrew 4:16)

We should be confident and claim our blessings from God. Life is not always smooth - we go through ups and downs every day. Even the people closest to God have had to endure tribulations in life. Jesus himself as the son of God endured a lot of pain and sorrow yet He was the son of God. Then who are we not to go through pain. It is said that we should be patient and kind to one another because everyone is fighting a battle that we know nothing about.

Joshua and Caleb are good examples of people that were optimistic and had strong faith and confidence in God's mighty works even when they were faced with challenges whose solutions they couldn't fathom. The two were among the twelve spies sent by Moses to explore the land of Canaan and its occupants. This was with an aim of strategizing on how to invade and subdue the occupants of Canaan. The ten spies reported that the occupants were huge people and could not be defeated. However, Joshua and Caleb reported the contrary. They admitted that the occupants were as big as giants but acknowledged that God was more powerful than them. Numbers 13. This is the kind of report that we need to give every time we are faced with big challenges that almost breaks us down. We should remember that God is bigger than our problems.

The strength we have is not measured by how strong we may seem, but by how many obstacles that we have gone through that made us stronger. It is always said that what doesn't kill you makes you stronger.

Every challenge that we go through in life, teaches us a lesson. From having lots of possession, valuables, wealth and power, to having none. There are lessons learnt there.

I asked God for strength, that I might achieve,
I was made weak, that I might learn humbly to obey.
I asked for health, that I might do greater things,

I was given infirmity, that I might do better things.
I asked for riches, that I might be happy,
I was given poverty that I might be wise.
I asked for power, that I might have the praise of men,
I was given weakness, that I might feel the need of God.
I asked for all things, that I might enjoy life,
I was given life that I might enjoy all things.
I got nothing that I had wanted,

But everything that I had needed.

Almost despite myself, my unspoken prayers were answered.

I am among all men most richly blessed.

A soldier's prayer

(Written by an anonymous confederate soldier, U.S civil war)

Someone once said that a business is still a business even when you create it at 68 years old. A university degree is still a degree even when it takes eight years to complete the course. Barack Obama became the 44th president of the United States at the age of 47 years while his Successor Donald Trump became president at the age of 70 years. Joe Biden became president at the age of 78 years old. The fact of the matter is that regardless of their ages they all became presidents. This shows that it doesn't matter how long it takes to reach your goal as long as in the end you still achieve it. We are different, we have different journeys, and none is like the other.

Another thing that we should realize is to look at success from a different perspective. *"Money is not the greatest*

> *We can't change it but we can choose to make the best of the lives we have.*

measure of success. There is no amount of money that can compensate for lack of character, honesty, compassion and genuine empathy towards other people."

Some live longer than others while some die younger than others. This is the reality of life and we can't change it but we can choose to make the best of the lives we have.

For my thoughts are not your thoughts and your ways not my ways Isaiah 55:8.

The story of Hannah in the bible is an inspiring one. For many years, the woman had been barren. Her co-wife, Peninah, constantly reproached her for many years that God had left her barren. Hannah went through a lot of pain, always crying and refusing to eat. In her bitterness, she prayed to God to have pity on her sorrow and misery. After so much suffering, God remembered her and blessed her with a son and other children thereafter. (1 Samuel 1)

Many are the times we go through a lot of suffering and even become a laughing stock to other people. We end up thinking that God has forgotten us or we have even been cursed. What we need during such trying times is to lay our foundation of faith in God. God is happy when we have enough faith to go through our difficult times. He knows that through faith we still believe in his power to change things, to turn around our lives so that a bigger testimony of His glory can be seen in our lives. Let us keep close to our hearts the things that are good and harmless because, ***"Out of our hearts the mouth speaks"***.

10

REJECTION, OPPRESSION, AND FORGIVENESS

Rejection is always painful. No one loves it, be it from family, friends, spouse or even in schools and working environments. People deal with rejection uniquely. Some lose confidence in themselves; others fall into depression, others exhibit withdrawal symptoms and others even harbour suicidal thoughts. This could be an excuse to give up in life or live life miserably, but rejection may not always be harmful. How we choose to deal with it is what makes us different. Charles R. Swindoll once said, **"*Life is 10% what happens to you and 90% how you react to it.*"**

We may have our fates already defined, such as where we were born or which family we come from, besides that, we have our own free will to make our choices in life. We have the liberty to choose what we want to become of us in our present and the future of our lives. We have the choice to become responsible over how to react to events happening in our lives.

In whatever we do, we should always change our hurt from rejection into a source of motivation. ***"Put your heart, mind and soul into even your smallest acts. This is the secret of success"***- by Swami Sivanada. The first changing points of ourselves after experiencing rejection will always be our minds. First, you need to take charge of the situation. Instead of beating yourself up and feeling that, you are not good enough. Take it as another chance of improving yourself. Build up more confidence than before, take it as a motivation to aim higher.

On experiencing rejection, it gives us an opportunity to convert the disappointments into motivation to be better, in order to soar to greater heights.

Rejection could sometimes mean a diversion path that we need to take another course. There are times we may keep insisting on a path that we may need to divert from. This might also be a nudge to try your luck elsewhere or maybe improve yourself before trying again.

"As you come to Him, the living stone- rejected by humans but chosen by God and precious to Him" (1 Peter 2:4). Remember, you are precious to your creator, the one who created you in his own image and He has a purpose for you.

I know that when a door closes, it may feel like all doors are closing. A rejection can feel like everyone will reject us. But

a closed door leads to clarity. It's really an arrow. Because we cannot go through that door, we will go somewhere else. That somewhere else is your true life." (Tama J. Kieves)

Many are the times we get to hear of the phrase that we should forgive those who hurt and reject us. It might seem difficult but it is indeed possible. In the same way, let's strive to have God in our lives regardless of the situation we are facing, whether we are happy or sad. We should not run to God only when times are difficult - during the sad and tough moments. We should not look for God only when we want something from Him. Let us endeavour to be in communion with Him, every minute of our lives. When we do so, the journey of life will not be easy but we will be assured of his presence in our lives and He will be there to hold our hands and give us strength in our difficult moments in life and the promise of God shall come to pass. *"When you go through deep waters, I will be with you. When you go through rivers of difficulty, you will not drown.* Isaiah 43:2 (NLT)

> *The will of God will not take us where the grace of God cannot sustain us.*

The will of God will not take us where the grace of God cannot sustain us. - Billy Graham

Many are the times that people will reject you. They will want to harm you and may even succeed in harming you and hurting you, but in the end, God will make it up for you, for the survival of your future, your race and your people.

"Not only so, but we also glory in our sufferings, because we know that suffering produces perseverance, perseverance produces character, and character, hope. Hope does not put us to shame, because God's love has been poured out into our hearts through the Holy Spirit, who has been given to us" Romans 5: 3-5.

Take an example of Joseph who is one person in the bible that faced many challenges in his life and his faith was really tested in God. He almost perished as a result of rejection, persecution and jealousy from those close to him including his family, because of his ability to foretell dreams that seemed to show off his superiority over his brothers. He was betrayed by his family, his own blood brothers, who had plotted to kill him. They later resolved to sell him as a slave to the Ishmaelites who were on their way to Egypt. At that time, it was easy for Joseph to give up in life. However, God had a bigger and better plan for him and his future.

"When I am alone, God is my comforter. When I am nothing, God is my everything. When I am sad and lonely, God is my song and joy. When I am weak and helpless, God is my strength." - Anonymous

God was with Joseph even as he worked as a slave in Egypt and when he was thrown in jail after being falsely accused by his master's wife. In all these tribulations, God worked them for his good. He later became the governor of Egypt and rescued his race from the seven-year famine that they faced. His dreams came true, in that his brothers became his servants and bowed before him, just like in his other previous dreams. Additionally, one thing to note is that despite all that Joseph went through, he still managed to forgive his family for the sake of the peace, continuity of his family and their generations. At the event where their father died, his brothers feared that Joseph might still be holding a grudge because of the wrong things that they had done to him in the past. On the contrary Joseph had let go his past and had genuinely forgiven them for all the things done to him. He said to them, ***"Do not fear, Can I take the place of God? Even though you meant harm to me, God meant it for good, that he might exalt me, to achieve this present end, for the survival of many people. I will feed you and your children"*** Gen. 50:19-21.

Joseph was now in a higher position with so much power and wealth over his brothers and their whole family.

"When you walk through the fire, you will not be burned, the flames will not set you ablaze." Isa. 43: 2

Joseph had the freedom, power, wealth, and authority to do whatever he wanted with his brothers after his father's death. On contrary, he chose the path of peace. He chose to forgive them and to be merciful to them no matter what he went through in the hands of his brothers. He saw a bigger picture in the future for the restoration of peace, unity and continuity of their family generations, rather than dwelling in negative emotions and feelings of revenge towards his brothers' wickedness.

"The most beautiful people we have known are those who have known defeat, known suffering, known struggle, known loss, and have found their way out of the depths. These persons have an appreciation, a sensitivity, and an understanding of life that fills them with compassion, gentleness, and a deep loving concern. Beautiful people do not just happen" Elizabeth Kubler Ross - A renowned psychiatrist and bestselling author.

Many are the times in which we find ourselves that even after God has vindicated us from the long periods of rejection, pain and suffering, we would want to take revenge on those who hurt us and made us suffer. It is human nature to feel this way, but we learn from Joseph, that it is not necessary for this revenge, that we can grow bigger hearts and choose to forgive others and to forgive ourselves for the sake of peace, forgiveness and inner healing of our hearts, families and the society at large.

"For the God of all grace …will himself restore, confirm, strengthen and establish you after you have suffered a little."
1 Peter 5:10

You might suffer for a long time, many months and many years in life but remember that God has a way of restoring the wasted and lost years in your life.

"No future without Forgiveness".

I will restore back to you the years the locusts have eaten, the great locust and the young locust, which my great army had sent to you. You will have plenty to eat, until you are full, and you will praise the name of the Lord your God, who has worked wonders for you, never again will my people be shamed. Joel 2:25-26

Even in our lowest moments in life, we should remember that where God removes, he replaces.

The South African Nobel Peace prize winner Desmond Tutu talks of *"No future without Forgiveness".* In this particular book, he addresses on the years of suffering of his people who faced oppression, racial segregation, and rejection by colonialists, during the apartheid years (1948- early 1990s) in South Africa. He talks about the journey of forgiveness, which is a process that takes a day at a time, moment by moment. Forgiveness is painful and difficult especially for a historically oppressed people, who finally after many years achieve forgiveness by acknowledging the past and understanding multiple perspectives of life.

"Without Knowledge, there can be no forgiveness". "Life must go on and reconciliation is a process". Without knowledge on life, and new perspectives, it is easy to reopen past wounds that create anger and resentment towards one another. These are words of a woman named Jaqueline from Rwanda, who met the man that killed his whole family during the Rwandan genocide period in the year 1994 in Rwanda. Written from an article by Robert Bosch, It was not easy for her to forgive the man who wiped out the entire generation of her family before her eyes. It was not easy, it was a process, but the woman eventually forgave him. They now live peacefully as neighbours, helping one another in times of need.

Forgiveness is an act of love for our own selves. It allows us to feel the peace of mind and joy in our hearts again. This love for ourselves is called forgiveness, and has to be a conscious and deliberate effort to allow us to feel the freedom and a lifting of the burden from our hearts, the burden of anger and pain.

"Keep in mind that forgiving is not for others. It is for you. Forgiving is not forgetting. It is remembering without anger. It frees up your power, heals your body, mind and spirit. Forgiveness opens up a pathway to a new place of peace where you can persist what has happened to you." - Les Brown

Sometimes we will find that life is too short to waste time on grudges that we carry because others have not been good to us. In the moments that we carry these emotional burdens, we waste a perfect opportunity to enjoy and to be happy. Sometimes it may happen that those who have hurt us may have already made their ways right with God and asked for forgiveness from Him, yet on our side we continue to linger around with bitterness, hatred and unforgiveness.

"For at least there is hope for a tree, if it is cut down, it will sprout again, and its new shoots will not fail. Its roots may grow old in the ground and its stump may die in the soil, but yet at the scent of water, it will bud and put forth shoots like a plant" Job 14:7-9

Anger management is another life skill that we need for purposeful living in our lives. Anger is an intense emotional state of response that can be sometimes uncontrollable and is mostly triggered by hurt, provocation or a threat. The consequences of anger can be serious and damaging to our lives without proper management. Without control of anger, we may find ourselves in situations that become irreversible such as speaking words or acting in a manner that becomes irreparable. Since we are all human, we may find ourselves in situations of disagreements or differences of opinions. In such situations, some people might behave inappropriately that may trigger anger or stress. It is important for people struggling with anger issues, to make a conscious decision towards proper anger management. This is first realized by accepting that you may have a problem controlling anger. Most of us are witnesses of issues that have progressed from bad to the worst as a result of extreme anger. Once you have accepted that you have the problem, then make a conscious decision to take timeout to release the tension and to calm down before approaching the situation at hand. This is a process that is not achieved in a day but definitely gives progress with practice and a deliberate decision to embark on controlling anger and its proper management. If the anger situation is advanced, it is advisable to seek help from the relevant therapists.

Cast your burdens unto the Lord and He will surely give you rest in your heart. Talk to someone you trust if you need to. Join focus and help groups and listen to the experiences of others. You will be surprised that people have been through more tribulations than you have. Your problem might seem huge until you listen to others and find out that your problems are nothing compared to what others have gone through. Moreover, no problem is too great to be solved, when shared with the right people. So, take your time to laugh and rejoice when you can. Apologise when you make mistakes and let go of things that you can't control. Life is too short to be unhappy. We have to take the good and the bad moments altogether, none of them lasts forever. People and things will change and sometimes disappear, but remember in the end, life must move on.

11

HUMILITY, FAITH, GRATITUDE AND PEACE

The importance of humility in our day-to-day lives

Clothe yourselves with humility in your dealings with one another, for God opposes the proud, but bestows favor on the humble. Humble yourselves under the mighty hand of God, that he may exalt you in due time. Cast all your worries upon him because he cares for you. 1 Peter 5:5-7

Let's be humble enough in order to learn great things in life. Pride will prevent us from learning the lessons that we need to equip ourselves with for the future. *"Being humble means recognising that we are not on earth to see how important we can become, but to see how much difference we can make in the lives of others."* - Gordon B. Hinckley

Sometimes God needs us at our lowest and at the bottom most part of our lives to equip us with strength, courage and determination in order to prepare us for the highest and top most positions of our lives. God knows that we cannot learn when everyone is praising us and when we become the talk of town. Therefore, sometimes humility becomes a way of God using us as a vessel for His own Glory.

Sometimes God has to work on us first before he works on a solution - Rick Warren.

"I will not cause pain without allowing something new to be born." (Isaiah 66:9)

For every ministry to be born, there will be tears, sacrifice and pain. There will never be anything good and great that will be handed on a silver plate, even God himself had to sacrifice his own son so that humanity would be saved and redeemed.

Do we have enough faith to believe in God's promises? The Lord is pleased with people who have faith and complete trust in Him. Faith moves the heart of God. You may 

be in situations that you can't comprehend in your life. Everything may seem shattered, but He is asking you today to lean on Him, to trust Him completely with your heart and mind. To recognize and acknowledge Him without relying on your wisdom or understanding and He shall surely lead and direct your paths. In these moments we will have to go through the process and be patient, remembering that God is preparing us for greater things.

Be still and know that I am God. Psalms 46:10. This verse contains a deeper meaning that we should stop worrying, trying to figure out, understand and control things, because God is already in control.

God's timing is indeed perfect; never too late, never too early. There is no timetable that we must all follow. Before humans' eyes, events in our lives may seem late or even early, but there are over 7 billion people on this planet! So what's early, what's late? According to who? Do not beat your chest up because you are on your schedule and things are on time.

Trust the wait. Embrace the uncertainty. Enjoy the beauty of becoming. When nothing is certain, anything is possible. - Mandy Hale.

Sometimes we may find ourselves in situations, where we feel as if God is too far from us or maybe He has deserted us. Even with the promises that he had given us, we feel that he forgot about them, or even taking too long to fulfill. Hold onto Him, trust Him more. It might seem that He is not fighting for us in our troubles and tribulations. However, in His silence He is working for us, so that in the end of the battle, all will see His glory, and we will look back and see the good He will have done for us, so we may learn to Glorify Him, because it is not by our might, but by His power. So let us have peace in our sleep and forget our worries because in the silence of God, He is working it for our good. Just because something has not happened or isn't working out for you doesn't mean that it will never happen.

Let us open our hearts to God and be humble enough to give Him a chance to work on us, and perform miracles in our lives.

When the time is right, I the Lord will make it happen. (Isaiah 60:22)

12

SELF-IMPROVEMENT

Self-improvement is an actual conscious decision to better yourself, as a result of internal motivation, external motivation or both. To succeed in life, we need to have a plan and the right goals in mind. Sometimes in life, we only get one chance to plan and invest in ourselves through personal development and improving ourselves. This gives us a clear focus on our life goals. Life may give us one chance to change our lives and we must always seize that opportunity once it is at hand.

A life of proactivity will give you better success results than a life of just being reactive. Proactiveness is the state of acting in advance before a future event happens. Being reactive on the other hand involves waiting for a future event to happen in order to react or try to control it. Proactivity and reactivity give completely different results in terms of evaluation and performance of most activities and occurrences. Being proactive will mean looking for opportunities, to succeed, for example actively looking for jobs by profusely applying for job opportunities, rather than being reactive by waiting for a job to find you without applying for it. Being proactive means planning for your long term and short-term goals. It means having a vision and objectives to meet and speculating of any problems that may occur, rather than being reactive to react on the problems when they eventually occur in reality.

Sometimes, we may find ourselves going to our social media pages in the morning, the minute we wake up and in evening before we go to sleep. In this case, we are able to see people's happenings, issues and priorities. This makes us start our mornings from a point of reactivity, reacting to other people's events and surroundings on social media, rather than being proactive and choosing to spend our ideal mornings and evenings the way we would like to. For example, listening to motivational articles and speeches, praying and meditation to give us a powerful start for the day ahead or a peaceful night when going to sleep.

> *Do not better yourself for someone else, do it for yourself.*

Most importantly, we need to improve or better ourselves for our own selves and not for others. Do not better yourself for someone else, do it for yourself. Otherwise, it may bring up contempt, if the other person isn't happy for you or doesn't appreciate it. Let us start yearning and also fall in love with the process of becoming the very best version of ourselves.

We need to have positive self-thoughts and avoid self-criticism. Learning to forgive ourselves when we make mistakes is vital. Let us give ourselves a second chance to learn lessons and start the process of self-development that cannot be underestimated for our self-growth, and achievement of our hopes and dreams in life. Commitment is key in all of this. The ability to make a commitment to ourselves to be better people and to be agents of positive change to our societies.

I have learnt over the years through experience that comes with age that discipline, consistency and determination in your work are tools for success. We may not like to do what needs to be done but the sacrifice we put in now in our work, may not be rewarded at the present, but will surely be paid off in your future.

We need to create a lifestyle of deliberate living as opposed to merely surviving. We need to choose to thrive rather than to survive. Thriving involves flourishing, a life with a purpose - life with an aim of consistently, doing the little things that need to be done every day with a focus on some kind of achievement. Somedays, this will prove to be hard to accomplish. However, other days it may get easier. What we need to do is to stay focused on our goals and get consistent on the things that need to be done to achieve our goals. That is what actually makes the difference between existing and purposeful living.

Working on yourself is a continuous process. Working on oneself needs to be all round wholesomely. A continuous improvement process on ourselves wholesomely, entails the mind, body, soul and the healthy relationships with others that surround us. This also involves letting go bad vibes, negative thoughts, negative talks, low self-esteem, self-criticism and basically all the negative baggage and setbacks that continue holding us back from moving towards where we want to go and what we want to achieve in life.

You need to improve yourself consistently to achieve good results. *You are what you consistently do, then success is not an act but a habit*. - Aristotle

There is one tool of continuous improvement that I find very helpful. This is "*Kaizen*", A Japanese word that means "*continuous improvement/ change for better*". This concept has been learned and adopted by many successful companies. It has enabled them to advance to the higher levels of their businesses, by incorporating a strong culture of constant improvement among their employees. The continuous improvement will take time, that may mean months and even years of hard work with a mindset that we can always make things better even when they seem to work well in that particular moment. Kaizen, involves strategies that are aimed at improving efficiency. This involves improving the ability to do things well, and successively, with a goal of being more efficient. This is to be practised in our daily activities and behavior at a personal level and at organisational or job setting.

There are many theories to personal development that basically entail the activities or actions that are aimed at improving our identity, self-awareness, our capacity to build and develop talents and abilities in the realization of our goals, dreams and aspirations. The commitment to personal development will most of the time encompass the mental, spiritual, emotional, physical, social and moral aspects of our lives.

Law of attraction

Life sometimes doesn't give us what we want, but instead gives us what we need to develop, to grow and expand. This is the law of attraction that needs purposeful living, which asserts that positive or negative thoughts bring positive or negative experiences into a person's life. The belief is based on the idea that people and their thoughts are made from "***pure energy***". A process of like energy attracting like energy exists through which, a person can improve their health, wealth, and personal relationships. (Whittaker, S. Secret attraction. Redden, Guy, "*Magic Happens*"). You are responsible for the energies you give and the energies that you receive, because both make an impact on you as an overall person. In these cases sometimes, we find that we attract who we are.

Let us develop a strong mind. There is power in our minds and thoughts. "***The Mind is like a muscle, the more you exercise it, the stronger it gets and the more it can expand***" - Idowu Koyenika. What we think we want is what we may attract in life. Let us feed our minds with positive thoughts, reset ourselves and be humble enough to learn new things, and develop our skills everyday. This will attract more gratitude in our lives, leaving less room to anxiety, worries, and negativity. Let us always renew our minds with **new targets and goals**, every time we achieve those that we had set before. This gives us a reason to wake up and strive every single morning. We are responsible for our own lives, our thoughts, our minds, our results, success and failures. Learn to challenge yourself in order to grow in all aspects of your life. "***To***

get something you never had, you have to do something you never did."

You also need to know and feel that *"**you are enough**."* Do not compare yourselves to others to an extent of making yourself feel that you aren't enough. Trust the process and the timing in your life.

There is a story on the powerful lessons from the Eagle, which we should always try to remember as a tool for our development and self-improvement.

1. Eagles fly alone or with their own kind.

   Life lesson: Associate with people who are your level, or whom you can help one another to grow.

2. Eagles have excellent vision and concentration.
   Life lesson: Focus - Work on each of your goals to accomplish.

3. Eagles feed on live food/meat. They don't eat carcasses.

   Life lesson: Don't waste your time beating a dead horse. Know when to say goodbye and let go. Keep things current and keep them moving.

4. Eagles love the storm. They welcome the challenge it brings, as it makes them stronger.

   Life lesson: Get excited about the storms in your life, Challenges bring opportunities.

5. Eagles test the level of commitment before engagement.

   Life lesson: It is wise to ascertain the commitment of people we intend to partner with, be it in personal or professional life - all aspects of our lives. Trust is important in relationships.

6. Eagles are masters of change management, from preparing the nest for their eggs to teaching the eaglets how to fly so that they can learn to be independent. It's not a pleasant process for the young ones but the mother knows they have to learn.

   Life lesson: We must not become complacent in life, clinging to the old and familiar life. We can only grow if we are willing to step out of our comfort zone.

7. Eagles have to make a painful decision of rebirth at around age 40. The re-birth involves the death of the old self. The eagles have to decide whether to die or to go through a painful process of rebirth, which will extend its life for 30 more years. This process involves the painful task of knocking out its own beak and plucking out its talons so that new ones can grow. This entire process takes about 5 months to complete. Life lesson: No pain, no gain. Many of us want success or change, but without sacrifice, hard work, disappointments and heartbreak that comes with it. To survive and grow, we must be willing to change. Sometimes we may even need to go a step further – a death of the old self and a total rebirth. Ending toxic relationships and workplaces, getting rid of destructive habits, thoughts, traditions and mindsets that no longer serve us.

13

THE CONQUEROR'S MINDSET

We need courage in life to fulfill the dreams that we have always hoped for. This courage does not mean that it is the absence of fear; it is the triumph over our fears. **Fear can be an obstacle to our accomplishments in life.** Every next level in your life will need a different version of you. You cannot be the same in every season, and level of your life, and sometimes the process will be painful, stressful, difficult, and self-isolating. Sometimes you may need to leave others behind because it will be your own journey. Sometimes you may need to meet and get along with other new people, which may make you uncomfortable - that is okay. We have to be prepared to move out of our comfort zones to succeed, and sometimes, it may require every ounce of strength in us, and the absence of fear.

> *Every next level in your life will need a different version of you.*

To achieve great things in life, we will be required to sacrifice our comfort for future benefits. The early mornings , late nights, few friends, less social life and oftenly being misunderstood. All this will be part of the process.

In this regard, you might be required to be your own cheerleader; not everyone will be there for you, not everyone will be happy for you. You must learn to push yourself harder to the limits and aim higher

> *In this regard, you might be required to be your own cheerleader.*

for your goals. Do not get used to being too comfortable. In some cases, we may be filled with fear, the fear of taking a new step in our lives, and pushing forward. We may have the fear of starting a new life, a relationship or a career all over again. In all these, we need to make a conscious decision to overcome the fear. To decide that you want something more than you are afraid of it. Big decisions will always come along with doubt, a feeling of incapability and sometimes not believing in yourself enough. In such moments, we must deliberately make huge steps to overcoming the doubts in ourselves and believing that we can pursue and make it through in anything that we set our minds on to achieve.

"With His love, He will calm all your fears." (Zephaniah 3:17)

Sometimes we are afraid of uncertainty, and the fact that we are not able to predict the future. We should therefore not let fear of the unknown to cripple us.

In Romans 8:31-39, God speaks of his love for us. By his love, we can conquer all things through Him. *"If God is for us, who can be against us?"* God demonstrates his love by not sparing even his own son. If he sacrificed his own son for us, will he then not give us everything along with Him? He goes along to say that nothing will separate us from the love of Christ, neither anguish, nor distress nor persecution, nor famine, nor danger, nor death will separate us from his eternal love. "We can conquer all these things through Christ that loves us."

We might lose trust in our nation's or the world's institutions and systems, or the worldly orders but we should never lose hope in ourselves to make a difference.

Sometimes we blame the system (the government, political and social systems) for the events happening to us, but we have an option of choosing how to react to them. You might find yourselves blaming everyone and everything else but not yourself. You may blame everyone else for your failures (your past, parents, relatives, family, colleagues, and bosses) but then take responsibility for your success alone. This should not be the case. We must take total control by changing our mindsets to bring and initiate the change by ourselves and to be focused on improving our situations.

God, even though I don't know what the future holds, You do. Nothing is impossible for You. There is nothing that I face that you cannot conquer, and no battle or fight that you haven't already won. So when I feel discouraged by events going on around me, remind me that You are in control. Nothing can separate me from Your love. Thank You! Amen. -Anon

LIVE, LAUGH, LOVE AND GOD BLESS YOU.

BIBLIOGRAPHY

- Atomic Habits- James Clear.
- Long Walk to Freedom - Nelson Mandela.
- Facing Mount Kenya - Jomo Kenyatta.
- No future without Forgiveness - Desmond Tutu
- Secret attraction- Whittaker S.
- Magic Happens- Redden Guy.
- NIV Bible
- Good news bible
- Catholic bible
- Thepositivedairies.com
- www.mindfithypnosis.com
- www.goodreads.com
- www.cdc.gov/flu/pandemic 1918
- www.spica.com
- https://ipfs.io
- https://www.patheos.com/blogs/christiancrier/
- Youtube

Abbreviation

- NLT - New Living Translation